Presented to

_____

by

_____

on

_____

To my husband, Bob:
Thank you for helping me raise our amazing children. —C. B.

To my husband, Anthony:
Thank you for helping me shine my light. —J. M.

My Mama & Me

Rhyming Devotions for
You and Your Child

TYNDALE KIDS

Tyndale House Publishers, Inc.
Carol Stream, Illinois

Crystal Bowman & Teri McKinley

Illustrated by Phyllis Harris

Visit Tyndale's website for kids at www.tyndale.com/kids.

Visit Crystal Bowman's website at www.crystalbowman.com.

TYNDALE and Tyndale's quill logo are registered trademarks of Tyndale House Publishers, Inc. The Tyndale Kids logo is a trademark of Tyndale House Publishers, Inc.

My Mama and Me: Rhyming Devotions for You and Your Child

Copyright © 2013 by Crystal Bowman and Teri McKinley. All rights reserved.

Cover and interior illustrations copyright © 2013 by Phyllis Harris. All rights reserved.

Designed by Jacqueline L. Nuñez

Edited by Betty Free Swanberg

Unless otherwise indicated, all Scripture quotations are taken from the *Holy Bible*, New Living Translation, copyright © 1996, 2004, 2007 by Tyndale House Foundation. Used by permission of Tyndale House Publishers, Inc., Carol Stream, Illinois 60188. All rights reserved.

Scripture quotations marked NIrV are taken from the Holy Bible, *New International Reader's Version,*®
NIrV.® Copyright © 1995, 1996, 1998 by Biblica, Inc.® Used by permission of Zondervan. All rights reserved worldwide.
www.zondervan.com.

Scripture quotations marked *The Message* are taken from *The Message* by Eugene H. Peterson, copyright © 1993, 1994, 1995, 1996, 2000, 2001, 2002. Used by permission of NavPress Publishing Group. All rights reserved.

Scripture quotations marked "ICB" are taken from the International Children's Bible.® Copyright © 1986, 1988, 1999 by Thomas Nelson, Inc. Used by permission. All rights reserved. *ICB* is a trademark of Thomas Nelson, Inc.

For manufacturing information regarding this product, please call 1-800-323-9400.

Library of Congress Cataloging-in-Publication Data

Bowman, Crystal.

  My mama and me : rhyming devotions for you and your child / written by Crystal Bowman and Teri McKinley.
    pages cm
  ISBN 978-1-4143-7973-9
1. Children—Prayers and devotions. 2. Mother and child—Religious aspects—Christianity. I. Title.
  BV4870.B695 2013
  242'.62—dc23

                                             2012048629

Printed in China

19	18	17	16	15	14	13
7	6	5	4	3	2	1

Contents

How to Use This Book

"Mama, I've got questions for you!"

How many times has your child rattled off a lengthy list of questions? Young minds are inquisitive and like to explore. Some of the questions children ask are simple, some are humorous, and others are difficult. When children are asking about faith-related issues, their questions can be especially challenging. Wouldn't you welcome an opportunity to offer good answers to your child's most important questions? This book will provide the tools you need to do that!

YOUR TOOLS

- The short rhyming devotionals in this book give you age-appropriate topics and biblical facts to help you have faith-based conversations with your child.
- The Scripture verses bring young hearts to the Bible, showing that God speaks through his Word. As your child becomes more familiar with the Bible verses, you can

leave out key words for him or her to fill in as you read the verses together.

· Each devotional includes a prayer that encourages little ones to talk with God.

· The entries end with a mama-and-child activity to do at your leisure. These activities help solidify the concepts taught in the devotionals and give kids a fun, practical, creative way to apply their faith.

WHEN TO USE THIS BOOK

The best time to use this book is whenever it fits into your daily routine. Choose a time of day when you are not rushed so you can devote yourself to reading, talking, and praying with your little one.

Whether you use the book with one child at a time or with several eager listeners, our prayer is that this book will foster many important and meaningful discussions. May God give you strength and joy as you encourage your son or daughter to follow him.

Keep [God's] words in your hearts and minds. . . .
Teach them to your children. Talk about them when you are at home.
Talk about them when you walk along the road. Speak about them
when you go to bed. And speak about them when you get up.

Deuteronomy 11:18-19, NIrV

Crystal Bowman and Teri McKinley

Can You Tell Me about God?

Mama, I've got questions for you.
Who is God, and what does he do?
How did God make the great big sky?
How did he put the stars so high?

Did God make whales and zebras, too?
Does God take care of me and you?
Is God close by me while I play?
I want to know these things today.

God Is Your Creator

The skies were made by GOD's command;
he breathed the word and the stars popped out.

Psalm 33:6, *The Message*

Our Devotion

God said the words, "Let there be light."
That's how he made the day and night.
With his words, God made the sky,
the trees and bees and geese that fly.

He spoke to make the land and sea.
He told the stars where they should be.
He made the grass and animals, too.
When God made people, his work was through.

Our Prayer

Dear God, thank you for making our great big world. Thank you for pretty flowers and puffy clouds. Thank you for making me, too. In Jesus' name, amen.

Fun Idea for Mama and Me

Look through a window or go outside. How many things can you name that God made?

God Is Your King

Our Bible Verse

The LORD is a great God, a great King above all gods.

Psalm 95:3

Our Devotion

God is great, and he is King.
He's in charge of everything.
He guides the stars in outer space.
He keeps the ocean in its place.

He rules the world all day and night,
and you are always in his sight.
He rules the land, the sky, and sea.
God is King over you and me.

Our Prayer

Dear God, thank you for being a kind King. I am so glad that you are in charge of the whole world. Help me to please you because you are my King. In Jesus' name, amen.

Fun Idea for Mama and Me

Using construction paper, have your mama help you cut out a paper crown. Ask your mama to write "God is my King" on the crown. Decorate it with markers, crayons, or stickers. Glitter and plastic jewels work great too! Wear your crown as a reminder of who your King is.

God Is Your Father in Heaven

Our Bible Verse

See how very much our Father loves us, for he calls us his children,
and that is what we are!

1 John 3:1

Our Devotion

God's your Father; he knows what's best.
He gives you times to play and rest.
He'll help you learn and help you grow.
He'll teach you all you need to know.

God loves kids and grown-ups, too.
I'm his child, and so are you.
When we believe in God above,
he loves us with a Father's love.

Our Prayer

Dear God, thank you for being my Father in heaven. I am happy
to be your child. I am glad that you love me. In Jesus' name,
amen.

Fun Idea for Mama and Me

Make a Father's Day card for God. Have your mama help you
write "I Love You" on the card. As you make and color your
card, talk about why God is a good heavenly Father.

God Keeps You Safe

Our Bible Verse

The LORD is the one who keeps you safe.

Psalm 91:9, NIrV

Our Devotion

God keeps you safe all through the day.
He watches as you run and play.
When you're at home or in the car,
God is with you where you are.

He keeps you safe all through the night.
His moon shines down to give you light.
Even through a thunderstorm,
God will keep you safe and warm.

Our Prayer

Dear God, thank you for protecting me and keeping me safe all
the time. Thank you for always being with me and watching over
me. In Jesus' name, amen.

Fun Idea for Mama and Me

Turn your Bible verse into a song! Use this tune: "The Wheels on
the Bus." Practice singing it five times so you can remember it
the next time you feel scared.

The Lord is the one who keeps you safe,
keeps you safe, keeps you safe.
The Lord is the one who keeps you safe,
all day long.

God Gives You What You Need

Our Bible Verse

God will generously provide all you need.
Then you will always have everything you need.

2 Corinthians 9:8

Our Devotion

Do you have food? Do you have clothes?
Do you have socks to warm your toes?
Do you have toys and books to read?
It's God who gives you what you need.

Do you have blankets on your bed
and a pillow for your head?
God gave you everything you see.
I'm glad that he gave you to me!

Our Prayer

Dear God, thank you for my home, my food, and my family.
Everything I have is from you. Thank you for giving me what I
need. In Jesus' name, amen.

Fun Idea for Mama and Me

Think of five things that God has given you. What is your most
favorite gift from God? Have your mama take a picture of it
sometime this week.

God Is Good

Our Bible Verse

The LORD is good to everyone. He showers compassion on all his creation.

Psalm 145:9

Our Devotion

God helps the squirrels find nuts to eat.
He helps the bees make honey sweet.
He helps the robins build their nest
so they can have a place to rest.

He makes it rain when the earth is dry
and puts his rainbow in the sky.
He wakes us with the morning sun.
Our God is good to everyone.

Our Prayer

Dear God, thank you for being good to all the animals and people that you have created. Thank you for the sunshine and the rain. I know you are always good. In Jesus' name, amen.

Fun Idea for Mama and Me

Use a piece of cardboard or stiff paper to make a picture of a clock. Have your mama help you cut it out. Put the clock in a place where you will see it often to remind you that God is good all the time.

Can You Tell Me about Jesus?

Mama, I've got questions for you.
Who is Jesus? What does he do?
Does Jesus care if I am sad?
Does he know how to make me glad?

Did Jesus live here long ago?
These are things I want to know.
And why did Jesus have to die?
If you can, please tell me why.

Jesus Is God's Son

Our Bible Verse

[The angel told Mary,] "You will . . . give birth to a son,
and you will name him Jesus."

Luke 1:31

Our Devotion

A baby came to earth one night.
A special star shone big and bright.
The angels sang the night he came,
and Jesus was the baby's name.

God showed his love for everyone
by sending Jesus, his own Son.
When Jesus grew to be a man,
he followed God's important plan.

Our Prayer

Dear God, thank you for loving all of us so much that you gave us baby Jesus. Help me to be thankful for your Son, Jesus, all year long. In Jesus' name, amen.

Fun Idea for Mama and Me

Listen to your mama read Luke 2:6-20 in the Bible, and learn more about baby Jesus being born. Pretend you are one of the shepherds who runs to see Jesus. What do you want to say to him?

Jesus Is Your Teacher

Our Bible Verse

The people were amazed at his teaching, for he taught with real authority.

Mark 1:22

Our Devotion

The people listened every day
to all that Jesus had to say.
As Jesus taught, the people knew
his words were wise and good and true.

Jesus taught them how to live,
how to love and share and give.
Learn from Jesus, then you'll see
how wise and happy you will be.

Our Prayer

Dear Jesus, thank you for teaching me how I should live. Help me
to understand all your wise words in the Bible. Amen.

Fun Idea for Mama and Me

Jesus taught people to share with others. Talk about some
things that you might be able to share. Choose one thing that
you can share, and share it with someone today or tomorrow.

Jesus Is Your Healer

Our Bible Verse

A large crowd followed him, and he healed all who were ill.

Matthew 12:15, NIV

Our Devotion

Jesus healed the deaf and blind;
he never left the sick behind.
When people couldn't walk or stand,
Jesus healed them with his hand.

He healed them from the inside out.
That's what his life was all about.
So when you're feeling sick or sad,
he'll heal your hurt and make you glad.

Our Prayer

Dear Jesus, thank you for healing people who are sick. Thank you for also healing people who feel sad on the inside. When I am sick or sad, I will pray and ask you to make me well. Amen.

Fun Idea for Mama and Me

Do you know someone who is sick or sad? Make a special card to give to that person. Pray for Jesus to help him or her get better.

Jesus Is Your Friend

Our Bible Verse

Now you are my friends, since I have told you everything the Father told me.

John 15:15

Our Devotion

Jesus is a friend to you.
He loves you, and he listens, too.
He keeps your secrets in his heart,
so talk to him—that's where you start.

You can pray or sing a song.
He is with you all day long.
He will always be your friend.
His love for you will never end.

Our Prayer

Dear Jesus, thank you for being my friend. You are someone I can always talk to. Thank you for listening to me when I pray. Amen.

Fun Idea for Mama and Me

Trace your hand on a piece of paper. As you point to each finger, name a reason why Jesus is a good friend. (You can use the devotion above for ideas.)

Jesus Is Your Helper

Our Bible Verse

I will not be afraid because the Lord is my helper.

Hebrews 13:6, ICB

Our Devotion

When you're afraid, just say a prayer.
Jesus can help you anywhere.
If something's hard for you to do,
talk to Jesus—he's there for you.

Jesus can help you do what's right,
like share your toys instead of fight.
If you have problems, big or small,
Jesus can help you with them all.

Our Prayer

Dear Jesus, thank you for being my helper. Whenever I need
help, I will remember to pray and ask you to help me. Amen.

Fun Idea for Mama and Me

Jesus can help you to do lots of different things. He can even help
you learn a Bible verse. Have your mama read the Bible verse to
you again. Now have her read the verse below, and see if you can
fill in the missing words. "I will not be _____ because the
Lord is my _____."

Jesus Came to Be Your Savior

Our Bible Verse

The Father has sent his Son to be the Savior of the world.

1 John 4:14, NIrV

Our Devotion

People do things that are bad.
We sin and make God very sad.
Sin is wrong and that is why
Jesus came to live and die.

Jesus saves us—this is true!
He can be your Savior too.
Jesus is alive today;
you can thank him when you pray.

Our Prayer

Dear Jesus, thank you for dying on a cross to save me from sin.
Thank you for coming to be my Savior. I'm sorry that I've done
things I should not do. Please forgive me. Amen.

Fun Idea for Mama and Me

Jesus died on the cross to be your Savior. Using a brown crayon
and some paper, draw a picture of a cross and color it.

What Does God Think about Me?

Mama, I've got questions for you.
Does God know what I like to do?
Do you think he knows my name?
Does he know my favorite game?

Does he ever think of me?
Does he know what I will be?
Does he think I'm someone great?
Tell me now—I just can't wait!

God Loves You a Lot

Our Bible Verse

The Lord's love surrounds those who trust him.

Psalm 32:10, ICB

Our Devotion

The greatest thing for you to know
is God loves you from head to toe!
He made you, and he knows your name.
His love for you will stay the same.

So when you think of God above,
remember his forever love.
His love is great; his love is true.
That's why he sent his Son for you.

Our Prayer

Dear God, thank you for loving me so much. Thank you for loving
all of me from head to toe! In Jesus' name, amen.

Fun Idea for Mama and Me

Cut out paper hearts and glue them in a circle to make a
wreath. On each heart, draw a smiley face to show that God's
love makes you feel happy.

God Knows All about You

Our Bible Verse

LORD, you have seen what is in my heart. You know all about me.

Psalm 139:1, NIrV

Our Devotion

Think about the things you like.
Do you like to ride your bike?
Do you like to swing so high
and watch the clouds up in the sky?

Do you like to spin around
or splash through puddles on the ground?
God knows what you like to do.
He smiles as he watches you.

Our Prayer

Dear God, I am happy that you know all about me and that you know what I like to do. Teach me all about you, too, so I can do the things you want me to do. In Jesus' name, amen.

Fun Idea for Mama and Me

Use an empty tissue box to make a special "Me Box." Glue a picture of yourself on the side of the box. Find pictures of things you like. With your mama's help, cut them out and put the pictures inside the box.

God Thinks
You Are Important

Our Bible Verse

Aren't five sparrows sold for two pennies? But God does not forget even one of them.
. . . So don't be afraid. You are worth more than many sparrows.

Luke 12:6-7, NIrV

Our Devotion

At times you may feel very small
and wish you could grow big and tall.
But God thinks you're a great big deal
no matter what you think or feel.

God listens to the little birds.
He'll surely listen to your words.
Anything you want to say,
shout it out to him today!

Our Prayer

Dear God, I know that you think I am important, and that
makes me feel good. Thank you that I am important to you right
now, even before I get big. In Jesus' name, amen.

Fun Idea for Mama and Me

Here is a fun fact: it takes about 150 pennies to make one pound.
How many pounds do you weigh? Have your mama multiply 150
pennies times your weight. How many pennies is that? God thinks
you are worth even more!

God Thinks about You All the Time

Our Bible Verse

How precious are your thoughts about me, O God.
They cannot be numbered! I can't even count them.

Psalm 139:17-18

Our Devotion

God thinks about you all the time,
like when you run and jump and climb,
and when you sing or sleep or eat,
or when you share a tasty treat.

He thinks about you when you play,
and when you put your toys away.
He thinks about you all day long,
so praise him with a happy song!

Our Prayer

Dear God, the Bible says that you think about me all the time.
That makes me want to think about you, too. Thanks for
remembering me day and night. In Jesus' name, amen.

Fun Idea for Mama and Me

Using the tune "The B-I-B-L-E," sing this praise song to God.

I'm happy as can be.
God always thinks of me.
He thinks of me when I run and play.
He thinks of me all day.

God Thinks You Are Special

Our Bible Verse

How you made me is amazing and wonderful.

Psalm 139:14, NIrV

Our Devotion

God made only one of you
who looks and acts just like you do.
He made your hair and feet and skin.
He even made your silly grin.

He made your heart and soul and mind.
You are the only you you'll find!
Look in the mirror—what do you see?
God made you just how you should be.

Our Prayer

Dear God, thank you for making me just the way I am. I'm glad
that you think I am special. In Jesus' name, amen.

Fun Idea for Mama and Me

Did you know that no one has the same thumbprint as you
do? In fact, all of your fingerprints are one of a kind. Get out
some watercolor paints or finger paint and a piece of drawing
paper. Create a picture that only you can make by using your
thumbprints and fingerprints instead of a paintbrush. When you
look at your one-of-a-kind artwork, remember that God thinks
you're special.

God Has Big Plans for You

The LORD says, "I will guide you along the best pathway for your life.
I will advise you and watch over you."

Psalm 32:8

Our Devotion

What do you want to be someday?
A nurse or soldier far away?
A firefighter or a vet,
a teacher or an architect?

God will show you where to go
and teach you what you need to know.
Whatever you may choose to do,
God will always be with you.

Our Prayer

Dear God, thank you that you have plans for me. I can't wait to find out what they are. I know you will help me do good things. In Jesus' name, amen.

Fun Idea for Mama and Me

Find a picture of a person doing what you want to do when you grow up. Have your mama help you cut out a picture of your face and glue it over the person's face. Tell someone this week what you want to be when you grow up.

How Can I Show God I Love Him?

Mama, I've got questions for you.
God loves me—I love him, too.
Should I tell him when I pray?
Will he know if I obey?

Does he know what's in my mind?
Does he want me to be kind?
Please tell me what to do and say
to show my love for God today.

Tell God You Love Him

I love the LORD because he hears my voice.

Psalm 116:1

Our Devotion

God loves to hear his children pray.
He listens to the words you say.
Just say, "I love you!" Don't be shy.
You can do it if you try.

Tell God that you love him so.
Your love for him will grow and grow.
He'll fill your heart up to the top
with love so great it will not stop.

Our Prayer

Dear God, I want to tell you that I love you. Thank you that you love me, too, and that you like to hear me pray. In Jesus' name, amen.

Fun Idea for Mama and Me

Using the tune "Mary Had a Little Lamb," sing to God about how much you love him.

God, I love you very much,
very much, very much.
God, I love you very much,
and I want you to know.

Obey God

Our Bible Verse

If you love me, obey my commandments.

John 14:15

Our Devotion

God's happy when you do what's right,
so try to please him day and night.
Try to do the things you should.
Try to do what's kind and good.

God will see your love each day
when you listen and obey.
Do your best, and it will show.
If you love him, he will know.

Our Prayer

Dear God, please help me to obey you. I know that when I obey,
you see how much I love you. In Jesus' name, amen.

Fun Idea for Mama and Me

Listen to your mama read Luke 10:27 in the Bible. Jesus says
there are two important ways you can obey God. What are they?
How can you obey God today? How will you show love for someone
else?

Be Thankful to God

Our Bible Verse

Always give thanks to God the Father for everything,
in the name of our Lord Jesus Christ.

Ephesians 5:20, ICB

Our Devotion

Give your thanks to God above
to show your heart is full of love.
Be thankful for your home and friends
and all the good things that God sends.

Be thankful for each happy day.
Be thankful you can laugh and play.
Be thankful you can dance and sing.
Give thanks to God for everything.

Our Prayer

Dear God, thank you for being so good to me. Thank you for my home and my food and my family. Most of all, thank you for your love. In Jesus' name, amen.

Fun Idea for Mama and Me

Use paper, crayons, and glue to make a Thank-You Tree. Draw a tree trunk with branches on a piece of light-colored paper. (Or you can glue real twigs onto the paper if you have some in your yard.) On bright-colored paper, draw and cut out several leaves. On each leaf, draw or paste a picture of something you are thankful for (food, pets, family, flowers). Then glue the leaves onto your tree.

Be Kind to Others

Our Bible Verse

Be kind and loving to each other.

Ephesians 4:32, ICB

Our Devotion

Remember, it is always right
to say kind words and be polite.
Say "please" and "thank you" when you play,
and help to put the toys away.

Be kind to someone who is sad,
and hug your friends to make them glad.
Do your best to help and share.
Be kind to others everywhere.

Our Prayer

Dear God, please help me to be kind to others the way you are
kind to me. Help me to use kind words with my friends and
family, and teach me to be polite. In Jesus' name, amen.

Fun Idea for Mama and Me

You can be extra kind to someone this week! Choose from one of
the ideas below, and then tell your mama when you do it:
- Help your friends, brothers, or sisters pick up their toys.
- Put the napkins on the table before mealtime.
- Give someone a hug and tell that person you love him or her.

Think about Good Things

Our Bible Verse

If anything is excellent or worthy of praise, think about those kinds of things.

Philippians 4:8, NIrV

Our Devotion

In the sky and on the ground,
God made good things all around.
Think about the mountains tall
or tiny snowflakes as they fall.

Think about God's love for you
and how his promises are true.
Read the Bible, sing, and pray.
Think of good things every day.

Our Prayer

Dear God, help me to think about all the different things you
have made. Help me to think about what you say in the Bible.
Thank you for giving me lots of good things to think about. In
Jesus' name, amen.

Fun Idea for Mama and Me

Play a Good Things thinking game together:
- Name two good things that God put in the sky.
- Name two good things that God put on the ground.
- Name two good things that God tells us in the Bible.

Take Care of God's World

Our Bible Verse

You made human beings the rulers over all that your hands have created.
You put everything under their control.

Psalm 8:6, NIrV

Our Devotion

You can help, and you can care
for God's creation everywhere.
Water the flowers in your yard.
Pick up the trash—it isn't hard.

Plant a tree and watch it grow.
Catch a bug and let it go.
Be kind to creatures that you see.
God put them here for you and me.

Our Prayer

Dear God, thank you for making such a beautiful world for me to
live in. Help me to take good care of everything you have made.
In Jesus' name, amen.

Fun Idea for Mama and Me

Listen to your mama read the story of Creation from the first
book in the Bible (Genesis 1). Does knowing that God created the
world make you want to take care of it? Which parts of God's
world can you help take care of?

Tell Others about God

Our Bible Verse

God . . . I will tell everyone about the wonderful things you do.

Psalm 73:28

Our Devotion

Because you know that God loves you,
tell others that he loves them, too.
Tell your friends he's always near.
Say it loud for all to hear!

Tell them God is good and kind,
and he's the best friend they will find.
Talk about the things he's done,
like sending Jesus Christ, his Son.

Our Prayer

Dear God, help me to tell others about you and how much you love
them. I want my friends and everyone else to love you as much as
I do. Thank you for being a great God! In Jesus' name, amen.

Fun Idea for Mama and Me

Use heavy paper or a file folder to create a bumper sticker. Have
your mama cut it to the size you need and print the words "God
Loves You!" on the paper. Draw a heart around the word *Loves*,
then color the letters. Tape your bumper sticker to a riding toy or
bike. Point to the bumper sticker and tell everyone, "God loves you!"

A Mother's Prayer

I could have no greater joy than to hear
that my children are following the truth.

3 John 1:4

Dear Lord, please bless my children
in everything they do.
As they grow and live each day,
please keep them close to you.

Watch them as they run and play,
and calm their childish fears.
Comfort them when they are sad,
and wipe away their tears.

I pray that they will know you
as a Father and a Friend.
Help them to appreciate
the blessings that you send.

Please protect their innocence;
keep evil far away.
Give them faith to trust in you,
and help them to obey.

Teach them, Lord, to know your will.
Direct the steps they take.
Give them wisdom from above
for choices they must make.

Give me patience, strength, and grace
to be a godly mother.
Fill our home with happiness
and love for one another.

Help our family to be strong,
to do our very best,
that others may see Christ in us
and know that we are blessed.

When my children reach the age
to go out on their own,
I pray they'll walk beside you
and know they're not alone.

Amen.

About the Authors

Crystal Bowman is a bestselling author of over seventy books for children, including *The One Year Devotions for Preschoolers*, *My Grandma and Me*, and *My Read and Rhyme Bible Storybook*. She has written numerous I Can Read! books, as well as stories for *Clubhouse Jr.* magazine and lyrics for children's piano music. Crystal is a mentor and speaker for MOPS (Mothers of Preschoolers), and she also speaks at churches, schools, and writers' conferences. Whether her stories are written in playful rhythm and rhyme or short sentences for beginning readers, her desire is to teach children that God loves them and cares about them very much. Crystal and her husband live in Florida and have three married children and one granddaughter.

Teri McKinley grew up in the world of publishing, attending book signings and book conventions with her mother, Crystal Bowman. She began writing stories in elementary school, and her love for writing grew in college while attending Baylor University. She has been published in national magazines such as *SUSIE Magazine* and *The Eleusis*, and has also written greeting cards for Discovery House Publishers. She has a master's degree in Interior Design from Arizona State University and currently works as a student adviser at a Baptist university. Teri and her husband live in Texas.